Shuttlesworth: J40   333.7
DISAPPEARING   ENERGY   SHU

DATE DUE

Disappearing Energy

Disappearing Energy

Can We End the Crisis?

**by Dorothy E. Shuttlesworth
with Lee Ann Williams**

Doubleday & Company, Inc., Garden City, New York

Acknowledgment: The appreciation of the authors goes to Gregory J. Shuttlesworth, Energy Economist, for a critical reading of this manuscript, and an exchange of ideas on energy problems.

Library of Congress Cataloging in Publication Data

Shuttlesworth, Dorothy E
    Disappearing energy.

    SUMMARY: Discusses the sources of energy, their rapid depletion, and ways of conserving them.
        1.   Power resources—Juvenile literature.
    2.   Energy conservation—Juvenile literature.
    [1.   Power resources.   2.   Energy conservation]
    I.   Williams, Lee Ann, joint author.   II.   Title.
TJ153.S57   333.7
ISBN 0-385-04862-9 Trade
        0-385-04863-7 Prebound
Library of Congress Catalog Card Number 73–20943

9   8   7   6   5   4

For our Melissa
a most delightful "bundle of energy"

Contents

1. The Problems of a "Good Life"

Energy is the most important thing in the world. It is the ability to work and grow. It is the cause of all motion and change. But because we cannot see an "ability" or a "cause," energy is not easily understood.

Where does energy come from? How does it function? Why are we worrying these days about its disappearance?

The answers to these apparently simple questions are not simple in themselves. The energy of our own bodies may be said to come from our food. Energy to make plants grow involves soil and water. The energy needed to create the electricity that powers the countless mechanical devices of today's world involves other natural resources —coal, gas, and oil—while uranium is needed for nuclear energy.

And behind all the energy of living things, as well as mechanical energy, is the sun.

Because of sunlight, plants can convert inorganic materials into organic. Plants are the basic food of all animal life. They also contribute to the air we breathe, for plant growth creates oxygen.

Not only is solar energy responsible for good air and food, it creates our water supply. The sun's heat is constantly drawing water out of the salty seas, leaving the salt behind. Winds blow much of this fresh water over land areas where it comes to the earth as rain or snow.

Many thousands of years ago these things—sun, air, water, plants—were all that existed to support animal life and the needs of people. Not a single machine existed. Electric light, candlelight, and even firelight were unknown.

Yet people managed to live. They obtained food, shelter, and clothing simply by using their own human energy for hunting edible plants and animals, for settling into cave homes, and for making wearing apparel from animal skins. Their hands were their tools. Eventually, as they learned to harness and use energy other than that of the human body, inventions began to change the ways of the world, and they talked proudly of their "progress."

But progress brought problems. For a while everyone seemed delighted with the steady stream of new inventions, and then with faster automobiles, bigger airplanes, brighter lights, and more luxurious homes. All helped to create a more interesting life, with an abundance of leisure and recreation.

Then, quite suddenly, an "energy crisis" developed and people were told they would have to cut down on the use of many things they had learned to enjoy.

Such a change in attitude was not sudden with everyone, however. For a number of years some scientists and conservationists had been worried about the disappearance of our natural resources, combined with a steady rise in the earth's population. They said the combination could bring about real disaster.

More often than not such warnings were ignored. But a number of facts bearing out the predictions became too obvious to be brushed

Once upon a time people enjoyed getting away from crowds by going to a beach. Today it is different; with an ever-expanding population, there often seem as many people as grains of sand. (Wide World Photos)

aside. Simple arithmetic explained the startling increase in population. If, three generations ago, there were four children in a family, all of whom married and had four children, there would be sixteen "second generation" cousins. If each in this group married and each had four children, there would be *sixty-four* people replacing, in a sense, the little family of four—all of whom might still be living. Not only are children multiplying each year, but people are living longer than they did a few generations ago.

With ever-increasing populations we see small towns becoming cities, and big, overcrowded cities sending out countless residents to country areas where land is then cleared for homes, markets, stores, and industry. All of which calls for more electric power, building materials, home furnishings, water supplies, and transportation.

Of course this is a drain on natural resources! Yet few people are willing to give up their conveniences. Comfortable heating in winter

There are people still living who can remember when this area of New York included trees, grass, and attractive homes. In today's crowded world it serves industry and business. (Wide World Photos)

and air cooling in summer, several television sets and radios in one home, freezers and refrigerators, one or more cars to every family, motorboats, and dazzling lights to brighten public places—such has become the picture of a good life in the United States. And every one of these things takes energy.

Tourists from the United States to distant countries are often surprised by the dim appearance of shops during the day. Are they really open for business? The windows and interiors seem too dark to be inviting. But, it turns out, the supply of electricity in these areas simply is not great enough to permit bright illumination all day and through the evening. To the native residents dim lighting is normal and acceptable. However, visitors from lands of unrestricted electricity are apt to feel it shows a lack of progress.

But today it seems some aspects of "progress" must be looked at from a new point of view. This does not mean we are doomed to move backward or to live dull, unimaginative lives. It does mean we must carefully examine our world, its population, and its natural resources.

Then we must plan. We must be interested in the ways some lawmakers and leaders of industry are trying to solve energy problems. And we must be careful to support changes that "make sense," not accepting new suggestions until they have been thoroughly investigated. Sometimes changes solve one problem but, by doing so, create others.

And we must be familiar with those gifts of nature—our natural resources. Only they can supply the energy we must have for a good life—or, in fact, any life at all.

Electric energy almost turns night into day in great cities such as New York. (Ewing Galloway Photo)

2. At the Flick of a Switch

Naturally, when we think of energy, we think of electricity. How much can happen when we flick a switch or push a button! Lights may go on—a motor starts—an elevator goes up or down—a fan, a toaster, a radio, or a television set operates. And all because of electric power.

When there is a power failure, bright lights and all electrical services vanish in seconds. This picture taken during a "blackout" along the eastern seaboard of the United States shows a few of the millions of people trapped in darkness. They were able to find a small emergency light, but it gave them little comfort as hours went by. New York City had been brought to a standstill. (Wide World Photos)

When there is a power failure (caused by damage to utility lines or by electric circuits becoming overloaded) everyone realizes how completely our way of life depends on electricity. Everyone agrees it must be kept available for the future, and all are alarmed at the very thought of its disappearing.

Electricity is a complicated "something" to understand. When we see flashes of lightning, we know that electric discharges are leaping from one cloud to another, or from a cloud to the earth. We know, also, that electricity can be stored in batteries until a chemical change makes their electrical energy available to us. We see, with our lights and appliances, the results of electricity in motion, as electricity flows through conducting wires. We know that electricity combined with magnetism (creating electromagnets) makes possible, among other things, telephones, electric bells, radios, and televisions.

These few bits of knowledge point up the fact that although electricity is a natural force, it also is constantly being created to serve our needs. Therefore it is not a natural resource; it is, in fact, a user of natural resources, and should be considered a secondary form of energy.

To satisfy our country's electrical requirements today, the electric utilities consume about 25 per cent of the primary forms of energy—oil, coal, natural gas, and water—which are "disappearing" as time goes on.

An understanding of the possibilities of electricity and how it could be manufactured and controlled took hundreds of years. In ancient times lightning represented mystical power—perhaps of war-like gods who were believed to live somewhere in the heavens. It was not until the seventeenth century that its mysteries and other aspects of electricity began to have real meaning. Then a German physicist, Otto von Guericke, made an important contribution when he built a machine that could generate electric sparks, reproducing the light and crackle of lightning on a small scale.

During the next century, Benjamin Franklin's famous experiment with a kite further revealed, and brought forcibly to public attention, the similarity of lightning and the electricity that could be made by men. Franklin attached a sharp-pointed wire to a kite. Then, to the lower end of the kite's holding twine, he fastened a key and a few feet of silk ribbon. When a thundercloud passed over the kite, "electric fire" came down through the wire, down the twine, which was wet from the storm, and on out through the key. (Fortunately he carried out the experiment with great caution. Others who made the attempt were killed or badly shocked.)

Franklin then demonstrated that all the experiments he and other people had been performing with electricity that was created with man-made apparatus could be done also by using nature's electricity.

About this same time, an Italian scientist, Luigi Galvani, was researching the possibilities of electricity and found the basic principle of electric current, and how this remarkable force could be turned into flowing energy.

Electric current was the real beginning of electricity's enormous contribution to the world, although nearly a hundred years were to pass from the time of its discovery until its impact began to be felt. As late as 1870 streetcars in American cities were still being pulled by horses!

This interesting means of transportation was gradually replaced by electric cars, and by 1890 the electric "street railway" was taking its power from an overhead line, through a long pole.

Strangely, just as horses were beginning to lose their importance in man's working world, the term "horsepower" was added to his vocabulary. It was based on the ability of a strong horse to raise a five-hundred-pound weight one foot in one second. Soon the word was being widely used to indicate units of power. Today, one "electric horsepower" is equal to 746 watts.

Once electrical inventions had been started, they moved along rapidly. The great innovation of gas lighting was not very old before it began to be passed over for electric light.

Thomas Edison was the genius behind this development; his experiments resulted in the incandescent light. And on New Year's Eve 1879, a number of lighted bulbs were stretched on wires inside and outside his laboratory. Several thousand people traveled to West Orange, New Jersey, to see the fantastic sight. It was at this laboratory that countless other electric marvels were to be invented.

Of course the early light bulbs were primitive. Most of the electrically created energy for them was wasted as heat, instead of going to its real purpose—light. Then came neon lamps in which air is pumped out of glass tubes and a small amount of a rare gas, neon, is let in. An electric current is sent through the tube, and the gas glows with an orange-red color. Treated to a bit of mercury instead, the tube gives off a blue light. If sodium is vaporized with the current, a bright yellow light is produced.

A further advance was to send electric current through glass tubes filled with mercury vapor, producing a strong blue light, and also invisible ultra-violet rays.

Such lights, called "fluorescent," are more efficient than ordinary bulbs. They may change 30 or 40 per cent of the electric current into light, compared to a mere 12 per cent in ordinary bulbs. However, a fluorescent light does not work on an ordinary electric current without a transformer built into its base. This greatly steps up the voltage of ordinary house current.

Besides its progress with lighting, electricity took many dramatic roads until, today, it is looked upon as one of our most indispensable sources of power.

In what ways is all of it used? The greatest consumers are our in-

A generating station at night shines with the electric power it is producing for light and other electrical needs of its area. (Courtesy, N. J. Public Service Electric and Gas Co.)

dustrial plants. Forty per cent of all electricity generated in the United States is needed by industry. Home use, such as lighting and appliances, takes 29 per cent. Commercial buildings and spectacular lighting such as in shopping malls and advertising signs, use 19 per cent. The small remaining amount goes for such things as transportation and the process of transmitting power.

What makes it possible to generate all this electrical energy of more than a trillion kilowatt hours during a single year? The answer brings us to our disappearing natural resources.

3. The Giant Power of Water

If we watch a flooding river sweep away buildings, cars, and everything else in its path, we realize the tremendous power water can have. If we pay attention to the banks of even a gentle stream, we see how the moving water slowly but surely breaks down the soil and vegetation and carries it away.

Water indeed has power.

The people of several ancient civilizations found a way to make it work for them. They set big wheels, equipped with paddles, over streams so that the water would strike the paddles. Its force would turn the wheel, and power would be provided from it to grind corn or saw logs.

Such primitive water wheels served in the old Roman Empire. They were used in the Egypt of the Pharaohs and during ancient Chinese civilizations. But gradually they were neglected, and for many years were used only occasionally.

However, when colonists in North America were struggling to make a living, a few men had the brilliant idea of constructing a water wheel. They found an ideal spot to locate one—a creek near

Old-fashioned water-wheels did not generate a great deal of power, but they were helpful on farms—and they were picturesque. (Courtesy of the American Museum of Natural History)

Dorchester, Massachusetts. The water flowed at a steady pace, and there was a drop of about ten feet in the contour of the land. Here, in 1628, they built a dam of rocks and clay so that water would collect, ready to spill over the drop during dry seasons. At its base they set a large wheel with wooden water buckets attached to it at regular intervals. Water tumbling over the dam dropped into the buckets and, as a result of its force and weight, the wheel turned.

Water wheels soon became a New England landmark. Not only did they grind meal, they gave power for mill machinery to produce textiles. Little more than a hundred years later George Washington was so impressed by what he heard of the water wheels' accomplishments, he took time from presidential duties to visit a mill near Hartford, Connecticut. There he ordered enough cloth to have suits and dresses made for every member of his household.

The growing textile industry was rivaled by a booming lumber industry, as water powered one sawmill after another. The rapids in the rivers of Maine were ideally suited for the work, and the rich forests furnished lumber to be turned into ships. The ships then carried away cargoes of more lumber (prepared at the sawmills) to be sold at distant ports.

Water power was the foundation for American industry.

The "foundation" grew slowly for a number of years. Then the turbine was invented, and a mighty boost was given to increasing the efficiency of flowing water.

A turbine might be described as a "glorified water wheel." With the older type of wheel, the axis was parallel to the ground, so that the wheel was upright, and only a small part received a push from the running water at any given time. With the turbine, the wheel is set on its side, with an upright axis, and its construction involves a strong casing. As a result of its arrangement, the wheel receives the full energy of incoming water.

Another important change was the way the water hit the wheel. On the old type, water could not fall from a great height because the rather fragile structure of the wheel would be damaged. But with a turbine, the water hits the casing rather than the wheel. As a result, higher falls (providing more and faster-flowing water) can be used.

The first turbines were made of wood. Iron followed, then super-strong steel.

Turbines had been in use for about fifty years when, with a new invention, water was routed through a pipe with nozzles at its end.

From them, strong jets of water could be directed so that they would act most effectively.

With these inventions, water became recognized as a vast "natural resource," and when people learned to use it for generating electricity, its value was above measure. Hydroelectric (*hydro* in Greek is "water") plants became the great new means of producing energy.

It was a giant step from the first simple turbine to the high-capacity hydroelectric power system installed at Niagara Falls, toward the end of the nineteenth century, where millions of cubic feet of water tumble hundreds of feet every minute, day and night.

Until then, Niagara had been appreciated as one of the great beauty spots of the world. Afterward, with its new energy-producing equipment, it became known also as a center of power. Scores of industries clustered nearby, and its electric energy was transmitted across many miles to make still more industry possible.

The use of hydroelectricity soon spread over the world. In many European countries, in Asia and North and South America there was a rush to develop "cheap power" with water.

But natural waterfalls were not always to be found in places where power plants were desired. The next step, then, was the construction of giant dams, with their resulting cascades of water.

As with every natural resource, there is often a struggle for control between those who are interested in creating more and more industry and those whose greatest interest is saving our natural resources for future generations. In the United States when water power first became a leading source of energy, its development was in the hands of private corporations. Federal and state governments had little to say about how it was handled. Finally, in 1920, Congress passed a Federal Water Power Act which entrusted a Federal Power

Great dams, built to carry on the work sometimes done by natural waterfalls, also furnish water for irrigating the land. Here is a view of one of the greatest—Hoover Dam—on the border between Arizona and Nevada. It produces electric power, stores water for irrigation, and provides flood-control. It is more than 700 feet high. (Courtesy of the American Museum of Natural History)

Commission with the responsibility of issuing licenses for water-power development in navigable streams and on any public lands. From then on, water power became a governmental matter as well as being big business.

For a long time people were encouraged to use electric power. Lower rates were even established for those who consumed more than a certain amount, while consumers who used less paid at a higher rate. Electric heating became popular, adding to the need for increased hydroelectric power which already was furnishing energy for industry, commercial lighting, air conditioning, televisions, and countless other conveniences not dreamed of at the beginning of this century.

If we didn't give the problem much thought, we might suggest, "Build more power plants. What's wrong with that?"

Then we look at the daily paper and immediately see a story that suggests what might be "wrong." It is about an action taken by a County Environmental Council to prevent the construction of a power plant on a large bay. The Council pointed out that nearly one hundred acres of marshland would have to be filled in, thereby ruining the entire marsh—an area that serves several valuable purposes. Algae and plankton, on which ocean life feeds, are produced in it. It is a breeding area for fish and shellfish; it is a life-saving "stop-over" for migrating shore birds and a feeding ground for such mammals as raccoons and muskrats. If erected, the plant would require 230,000 gallons of water per minute during fourteen hours a day, five days a week. This would serve to cool machinery and it would then be returned to the bay. But its temperature would be eighteen degrees warmer than when it was drawn out.

An important question: How many such drastic changes can an environment stand?

Figures compiled by the federal government mention some startling water requirements for the country: In the early 1970s industrial needs in the United States called for 80 billion gallons a day. Municipal needs (part home, part industrial) required 17 billion gallons. The irrigation of farmlands absorbed 88 billion gallons. The report then predicted that by 1975 these water needs will have nearly doubled, or more than doubled. Industry alone will be requiring 215 billions of gallons a day.

Of course there are more elementary needs for water than making a turbine spin. People and animals alike must have it to live. We can die of thirst sooner than of hunger. Besides consuming water directly, we need it for the "chain" of energy which produces plants, which in turn become our food. And without irrigation, farms would long ago have failed in meeting the world's energy needs.

The use of water for irrigating farmlands is not so complicated as its use in developing industrial power. As early settlers pushed westward from the eastern states where water was plentiful, they found many arid regions. Soon they discovered they could make some of them productive by using nearby mountain streams. They simply directed the water to their gardens—and so the first irrigation projects in the United States were established.

However, as the population grew and greater quantities of food were necessary, small, private irrigation systems were not sufficient. Commercial organizations then began to handle such work, and state and federal governments became involved.

Irrigation on a large scale is not merely a matter of directing water into a dry area. Miles of ditches must be dug, and the land leveled, terraced, and otherwise prepared. Drainage systems must be planned. Today in the United States water, through irrigation, brings to life millions of acres that otherwise would be unproductive. On continents other than North America the story is the same. Huge irrigation projects have been constructed in Central Asia, South America, and Africa. All this, combined with the uses of hydroelectric power, gives support to a comment recently made by an engineer of the United States Geological Survey: "Water is the key of our present civilization."

When properly developed, irrigation projects and hydroelectric plants are a great team, because some of the water held back by a dam can be used for agriculture. But the facts about developments should be thoroughly understood because many people and much territory are affected by the way water is handled.

As rivers are manipulated to serve certain purposes, who is to say which purpose is best? Water taken to help in one area may be depriving another. An arrangement made to help in one existing crisis may create a greater problem for the future. And the people who are promoting projects may not be fully aware of the total situation, or they may be influenced by selfish interests.

In mountain areas where snow and ice fields at the summits furnish steady streams toward a power plant, the frozen water long ago became known as "white coal." This name is now often used for hydroelectric energy.

4. Coal — Past, Present, and Future

Not many years ago a science professor wrote: "If some wizard should, upon the first moment of an incoming year, banish all coal from the world, instant darkness would settle over the streets in most of the world's great cities. And their inhabitants would rise the next morning to find their houses cold and nearly all their factories motionless. The starvation that immediately faced them could kill millions of people before the next January."

This was at a time when coal was often called "black gold." Actually it was more important than gold, because it could provide energy, which gold could not. But when new means of creating power, such as hydroelectricity, began to make news, coal sounded rather old-fashioned. It seemed that perhaps some new miraculous inventions were going to take over the work that had been done by this fossil fuel.

However, quite the opposite is proving to be true. We find in current government publications such statements as, "United States coal

This mountain of "black gold" is a contrast to the old coal bin which held a fuel supply for a family or small business. But it is only a very small part of the enormous amounts needed by the electric light and power plant where it is about to be used. (Ewing Galloway)

29

reserves are expected to make a major contribution to meeting our rapidly rising energy needs, as well as providing an additional source when shortages develop in some of the other forms of energy. . . . Coal may be converted to liquid and gaseous fuels, including gasoline." At the time of crisis in the winter of 1974, many industries turned back from oil to coal for energy. Obviously this fuel belongs to the future as well as to the past.

Its "past" is a fascinating story which explains why we cannot hope for new coal to be made available as the old is used up. The process took millions of years. Today's supplies had their beginnings long before there were people on earth; in fact, even before the dinosaurs lived. It was a time when much of the earth was covered with dense forests which flourished in a warm climate and energy-giving sunlight. Huge fernlike trees, mosses, and rushes crowded together in swampy lowlands.

As the vegetation died, it fell into the swamps and soon it was covered with mud and water. Dying plants tumbled on top of those that had gone earlier, shutting them off from oxygen. Because of being shut off from air, the underlying vegetation decayed very slowly and, as a result, a high percentage of carbon remained in it. As ages passed, "mineralized carbon," or coal, was formed.

Pressure built continually on top of the decaying plants, and probably heat from the interior of the earth reached up to affect them. Chemical changes took place, and the more they were squeezed, the harder and drier they became.

In some areas where mountains were thrust up from flat regions, rock formations weighed heavily on newly formed layers of coal. This squeezed out any remaining water, and the result was our "hard" coal, called anthracite. When burned, it gives off practically no smoke or odor. Bituminous coal is commonly called "soft" coal, though actually it is not soft at all. It was formed by the action of low pressures while anthracite was subjected to harder pressures.

For many years coal was the most popular of all fuels for heating homes. However, by the 1950s, oil and gas had become available, and, to a large extent, were taking its place. They were more easily handled and were cleaner than coal. Electric heating was to develop later.

Only a generation or two ago, industries depended heavily on bituminous coal. It was the fuel that powered locomotives and steamships as well as manufacturing plants. And its value did not end with these early uses. Methods were developed for turning it into "coal tar"—a remarkable material that now goes into the making of hundreds of varied products—and into "coal gas."

When bituminous coal is heated in an air-tight furnace, gas and vapors result. These are piped off and cooled by water, and become useful for heat and power. A single ton of the coal can produce about 10,000 cubic feet of coal gas and approximately 120 pounds of coal tar.

Besides tar and gas, coke is formed in this process. It is left over after the gas and tar have been driven out of the furnace. It is harder than the original bituminous coal, and it is valuable in producing iron and steel.

Coal tar is a black, heavy liquid with an unpleasant odor. A young English chemist, eighteen-year-old William Perkin, thought the material would be interesting to work with, and soon he found he could make a purple dye from it.

This was about a hundred years ago. Soon other chemists were working along the same lines, and today nearly all dyes are based on ingredients from coal tar. Synthetic rubber, chemicals used in photography, plastics, sulfa and other drugs, nylon, and fertilizer are a few of the other products it makes possible. But with all these products involving coal, its greatest fame is as a source of power, and people who are aware of the world's energy needs now are anxiously asking, "How much is left?"

It is not easy to answer such a question about any natural resource, and particularly about coal. For years, estimates have been very much confused. When coal was first recognized as having great value, surveys were made in the United States—all too quickly, and often inaccurately. If any coal whatever was seen, without further investigation a whole county might be marked as "coal bearing." This sometimes was not true. And even where coal does exist, there is great variation in the thickness of the seams; they may be a hundred feet thick or only a few inches. Recording such figures was often a matter of guesswork.

Every continent has a share of the world's coal supply, but North America has been favored above all others in the quantity and quality of its coal. The United States has greater amounts than any other country.

Now experts are looking with new respect at a type called lignite. Compared with anthracite and bituminous, this coal has been rated "low grade." It is brown rather than black and has a high moisture content. When it is mined and brought into the air, it crumbles.

For years shipping and storing lignite was impractical because of its crumbling and the great bulk needed. In the United States it was unappreciated, while European countries were mining it on a large scale, and using it to generate electric power. But recently the Bureau of Mines has changed the situation in the United States by finding a way to convert lignite into a gas of high heating value.

While we cannot expect "real" coal to form during our lives, or for countless generations to come, there is a coal-in-the-making, known as peat, that also can be used for energy. Peat bogs are especially plentiful in Russia, Ireland, and other European countries, but the United States also has some. They are composed of materials which, under proper conditions, would become bituminous or anthracite coal after some millions of years. However, right now the peat can give valuable energy if it is turned into gas.

There are many giant steps between the discovery of coal in the earth and putting it to use, and unfortunately the abundance of American coal encouraged wasteful methods of handling it. Though it is possible, by proper methods, to secure nearly all of the existing coal as a mine is being worked, for years much that was available remained untouched when a mine was abandoned. Usually no more than 60 or 70 per cent of the "black gold" was taken out. And because of the financing involved, returning to a deserted mine was never considered worth while.

Coal is mined in several ways. Strip (or surface) mining is the easiest, but it can be carried on only where the veins are close to the earth's surface. Powerful blasts are used to break up the ground, then electric steam shovels scoop this up and away. Such operations are cheaper than underground mining, but it has scarred and destroyed countless acres of beautiful land.

Not long ago, in a single year, forty million tons of coal were taken by strip mining from eastern Kentucky. The result? Sediment falling into streams in the affected area was increased as much as thirty thousand times. Before long, not surprisingly, all fish were dead and water supplies for homes and small farms had vanished.

Some attempts are being made to persuade both the public and our lawmakers that strip mining is a great solution to our energy problems, because it is relatively quick and inexpensive. And the claim is made that all damaged land can be restored. Recently en-

Away goes the soil as a strip-mining operation begins. The bulldozer is scooping up earth, to a depth of about twenty-five feet, that lies on top of a coal seam. (Ewing Galloway)

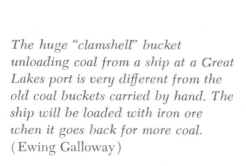

The huge "clamshell" bucket unloading coal from a ship at a Great Lakes port is very different from the old coal buckets carried by hand. The ship will be loaded with iron ore when it goes back for more coal. (Ewing Galloway)

acted federal laws require that this be done. However, the expense of such restoration will be fantastically high, and coal obtained by strip mining, as a result, will no longer be cheap. A close watch would have to be kept to make sure that strip miners live up to their obligations.

Coal is taken from deeper in the earth than by strip mining by digging tunnels with a gradual slope. But more often mines are great underground networks, with shafts, passageways, railways, and elevators. Rooms are cut into the coal seams, and thick pillars or walls are arranged to prevent the roof from caving in.

In 1960 an Office of Coal Research was established by the United States Government. Its functions are many; among them is researching every possible way to get energy out of coal.

One exciting development is a coal-fired gas turbine that produces electrical energy. This turbine may increase by as much as 10 per cent the amount of power generated by a given quantity of coal. Another project is aimed at converting coal chemically to electric energy, giving it greater efficiency than when it is converted by combustion.

Other possibilities for coal lie in its use in improving the quality of water, and also in making more water available for the creation of energy. Pulverized coal has proved to be a good filter in polluted water, cleansing it of phosphates that cause algae to grow too rapidly, thus robbing the water of its oxygen. Besides, when the pulverized coal becomes saturated with pollutants, it can be dried, then burned for the production of energy.

Coal energy can help to convert brackish water into fresh water, sometimes generating power as it does so.

When it is first brought up from underground, coal may look dull and "dead." But to see it burning and glowing is to appreciate its kinship with the sun which was responsible for its creation, and to realize its value as a creator of energy.

5. Gas — Natural and Man-made

A front-page newspaper headline in the summer of 1973 reads: "U.S Firms to Get Gas in Siberia." Its story explains a project in which the United States and Russia expect to bring, every day, two billion cubic feet of natural gas halfway around the world. It is to go through a pipeline from Siberia to the Pacific Ocean, then by tankers to our West Coast. Plans call for this operation to begin in 1979.

Pipelines take gas across the miles, sometimes through hills, valleys, and rivers. This one, about to be lowered into its trench, was laid to bring gas from Texas to Illinois. (Wide World Photos)

When natural gas was first being put to work, such a plan would have been thought impossible. Its use was limited to areas close to where it was found in the earth. But then great pipelines were constructed so that it could be brought almost anywhere it was needed.

Many people do not really understand the difference between natural and manufactured gas. If they open a valve on a gas stove or other appliance, it bursts into flame because of contact with a match or pilot light. There is no particular clue to indicate which kind of gas is serving them.

Natural gas is, of course, far older than any that is manufactured. As with coal, its history goes back millions of years, when it was created by the decaying remains of plants and animals. Various chemical changes took place as time passed, and rock formed around and above this mixture of materials.

Thus natural gas was formed and imprisoned in the earth in much the way oil was. Some people learned of its existence long before our industrial age began because it had worked its way to the earth's surface through natural openings. Thousands of years ago it was put to use in China, with hollow bamboo stalks serving as pipes. Gas moved through them to the ocean, and there it was burned. The heat that resulted evaporated sea water and, in this way, produced salt.

In modern times when natural gas was first appreciated as a source of energy, its discovery was often accidental; the workers who found it were actually drilling for oil. But hunting for gas is now an important activity in itself.

When a deposit is found and tapped, the gas usually rushes upward as it is released from the confinement of a comparatively small space. If the pressure is great enough, and it is a short distance to the area where it will be used, the gas may go on its own to the

"*Natural*" *gas—modern style—is created at a remarkable plant that began operating in 1973, the first of its kind in the United States. The gas is called SNG, or synthetic natural gas.* (Courtesy, N. J. Public Service Electric and Gas Co.)

planned destination. More often, however, pumps are used, and there may be compression stations to help move it along.

In the nineteenth century, when natural gas first caught the attention of scientists, almost immediately it had two important rivals: electricity and manufactured gas.

It was in England that a manufacturer, William Murdock, experimented with making gas from coal. He arranged pipes so that gas given off by burning coal would flow from a furnace into his home—a distance of seventy feet. There he used it for lighting. Just twelve years later, in 1804, he built a gasworks that supplied all the light for a cotton mill.

The development of gas lighting spread rapidly in England, and shortly after, it brought a new look to the United States when the city of Baltimore was brightened by gaslight. Soon it was being manufactured in many parts of the world.

There are several different methods of manufacturing gas. With one, bituminous coal is piled into a large oven, made red-hot by a fire at its base. As the coal begins to melt, it gives off a gas—a mixture of hydrogen, carbon monoxide, methane, and others—that burn easily. This moves through an outlet pipe from the oven into a collecting main about half full of water. The pipe is set in the water, and as the gas moves through, it is cooled, causing such impurities as tar and ammonia to become liquid. They remain behind while the gas continues on through several other pieces of equipment.

After a final operation to remove the last of its impurities, the gas is ready to be stored. At this point it is sometimes mixed with natural gas.

Along with electricity, gas became the foundation of our industrial age. And today with space exploration taking us into a new age of activities and discovery, it has achieved an unexpected importance.

Spotlights brighten the moon rocket, Apollo 17, as it is readied for a blast-off. Helium, an element of gas, is used in the launching. (Wide World Photos)

Its link to space travel is one of its elements—helium. Helium gives the thrust that ejects fuel to rocket engines; the spectacular "blast-off" follows.

This and many other uses had been found for helium before anyone realized how much of it was being wasted. As the natural gas of which it was a part was burned as fuel, the helium (which will not burn) was allowed to pass off into the atmosphere.

For some years the United States Bureau of Mines has been operating plants to prevent this waste. However, working as a federal agency, it did not have some of the advantages enjoyed by private industry. Then, in 1961, the government and industry arranged to co-operate, and within two years, five industrial plants were operating which delivered great quantities of helium to the government to be stored. It is estimated that by 1983 the government will have obtained more than 62 billion cubic feet of helium that otherwise would have been wasted.

6. The Wonders of Petroleum

Today anyone is likely to know one fact, if no other, about petroleum—that is, gasoline is made from it. This seems all-important, for gasoline makes automobiles and motorcycles run.

But petroleum has many other possibilities. It may be refined into solid form (such as paraffin) and gaseous form (such as "manufactured gas"), and distilled not only into gasoline, but other liquid products. It may even be burned in its crude state. It is used as a basis for the manufacture of such things as synthetic rubber, nylon, and detergents.

The history of the United States' growth into a great industrial nation is filled with stories about the discovery of petroleum, or oil, as it is more usually called. Overnight, millionaires were created when the dark, thick liquid suddenly gushed from a newly dug well, or was discovered oozing out of the earth in someone's back yard.

Such events began little more than a hundred years ago, although oil was known long before that. It is mentioned in the Bible as "slime," and it was reported by Marco Polo who wrote of a fountain "from which oil springs in great abundance." This was on the shores of the Caspian Sea where great oil wells are now operating.

Many centuries later, when explorers were investigating the North American continent, every now and then they found oil oozing from the ground. It was a curiosity and served some strange purposes, such as rubbing it on the body to cure rheumatism.

The first serious attempt in the United States to take oil from the earth was made in Titusville, Pennsylvania. The site seemed promising, but four months of work produced no results. However, when a depth of sixty-nine feet was reached, a black, oily fluid bubbled upward.

Edwin Drake, who had been employed to manage the operation, and his son immediately set a simple tin pitcher-pump in the well and began pumping. Soon they had brought up several barrels of the oil and they "rushed"—on muleback—with a sample, to the town a mile away where people had begun to make fun of "Drake's folly."

The time was right for the discovery, because by that year—1859 —the process of producing kerosene from coal had been well developed, and it was quickly adapted for making kerosene from oil. At that time kerosene was highly valued for heat and artificial light.

Today it is almost unbelievable that a hundred years ago kerosene was the most important product made from oil. The situation changed rapidly after the automobile was invented. Then gasoline was needed in ever-growing quantities, and oil for lubrication was essential for all kinds of motors. Other means of transportation— ships, trucks, and airplanes—soon joined in demanding gasoline for their internal combustion engines.

So the "oil rush"—similar to the "gold rush" of earlier years—was on. Many people began to buy small parcels of land simply on a

Before there were governmental regulations, derricks sprang up like mushrooms when oil was discovered. These, pictured near Long Beach, California, were removed some time ago, leaving the area covered with old oil pumps and tanks. (Wide World Photos)

hunch that oil could be found there. If some was located, they started to drill immediately. Such wells were known as wildcats.

Only a small percentage of wildcat wells really produced, and the system was extremely wasteful. A large pool of oil could be tapped by a number of such wells, set close together. Each landowner, therefore, would dig as many wells as possible on his own plot to get for himself the most possible oil. Fortunately such a practice was stopped some years ago when the government began to regulate the spacing of wells.

It is a tremendous jump from wildcat wells to the careful scientific studies being made today to decide where oil is most likely to be discovered, and then drilling for it as efficiently as possible.

Long ago a theory was suggested stating that oil had been created as a result of chemical action rather than from the remains of prehistoric life. However, advances in the science of chemistry made possible new discoveries about organic matter, and it is now agreed that oil is based in animal and plant life of long ago.

Over long periods of time, shallow seas covered much of our present land areas, and for millions of years rivers flowed into them carrying animal and plant life along with great volumes of sand and mud. All this spread over the sea floors, layer on layer, and the lower layers were gradually squeezed until they became hard rock.

Where numerous animal and plant remains were sealed off from air, and prevented from ordinary decay by the salty water, they turned into oil as well as gas.

Although all this happened under water, there followed great earth upheavals, and many areas rose above sea level to become dry land. So, today, oil may be found under water or far away from it. It is widespread, existing in many regions of the world, but certain conditions are needed to make it of commercial value.

The search for oil takes many forms. Here, during a survey being made offshore, a scientist checks the water's temperature with a "bathythermograph" for clues as to what lies below. (Wide World Photos)

For a really rich deposit, rock must have many open spaces which can hold oil. Then, somehow, the oil must move along into a reservoir and settle there. The underground reservoir cannot be porous or the oil would seep out again.

Sometimes oil does ooze up through faults in the rock to reach the earth's surface. And that is a situation where people may think they have found an "oil mine." But oil worth drilling for is rarely discovered by accident. And it is becoming harder all the time to find it, even with painstaking exploration. Recently the British Government spent 98 million dollars oil hunting in South Africa, only to find that, in spite of the existence of oil in the area, it was not abundant enough to be worth extracting.

A search begins with geological studies. Then test drills may be made, and equipment brought to the site to send down electrical impulses. Through electric waves, the investigators learn whether there is sand, shale, or limestone under the surface, and whether it contains fresh or salt water, oil, or natural gas. Or the testing may be done with dynamite, which brings vibrations to the surface, revealing the nature of things underground.

Even when great untouched supplies are discovered there may be difficulties in making use of them. An outstanding example of the complications that can develop is the case of the Alaska Pipeline—a plan to bring oil discovered on Alaska's North Slope to refineries on the West Coast and possibly other parts of the United States.

After the discovery of the great oil deposits, the Department of the Interior began a study as to how such a project would affect the environment. With a proposed route of nearly 800 miles, plant and animal life along the way could be threatened. Some oil might spill into waterways (the pipe would cross more than a hundred streams, including the Yukon River at a point where it is half a mile wide) destroying fish. And the extensive construction needed could have a harmful effect on mammal and bird life.

The proposal was for a pipe forty-eight inches in diameter. For hundreds of miles it would be placed in a trench eight feet deep and six feet wide. Above-ground portions would be supported by steel or by gravel pads. Twelve pump stations would be installed along the route to keep the oil flowing.

All this construction, and the maintenance after the building project was finished, would be quite certain to bring new chemical and biological materials into the territory—most of which belongs to the United States Government.

Obviously with the arguments against the pipeline on one hand and the need for oil on the other, decision making was tough and complicated. To help find the best answers, the Department of the Interior organized advisory groups made up of scientists and industrialists to investigate. After many months of study, in March 1972, a statement, filling nine large volumes, was issued. In it, all problems were weighed and ideas were suggested that might solve them.

Another tempting possibility for increasing oil supplies lies in the Continental Shelf—the submerged portion of our continent that extends from the shore to a point where a gradual slope drops sharply to great depths. Many experts believe that in these hundreds of thousands of square miles lie vast quantities of petroleum and gas.

Here again the government cannot agree to hasty action in allowing increased drilling. Offshore there are special environmental problems, because accidents of any kind in the water are likely to cause immediate, widespread pollution. Recent oil spills off California's shore and in the Gulf of Mexico are dramatic examples of the damage that can result. So, in spite of an "energy crisis," the greatest

An artist's drawing shows undersea activities in oil production. In this system, petroleum comes up through the legs of several "satellites." It then goes through flowlines to one central holding facility, and from there moves up to a processing plant that floats at the water's surface. (Wide World Photos)

care must be taken obtaining fuel in ways that could seriously harm water and the life it supports.

One possibility for new energy may be found in the form of oil shale—a sedimentary rock not very different in form from some types of coal. Millions of acres of land in the United States contain abundant quantities of it. However, the cost of mining and processing such rock—removing its fatty oil deposits—has never been able to compete with the cost of drilling for oil.

Now experts are giving a new look at this potential source of energy. But a number of legal questions must be settled before oil-shale lands become available for development.

By a mining law of 1872 the discoverer of a mineral could gain title to the land it was on for a small fee. He could then take the mineral from a mine without further payment to the government.

Up to the year 1920 oil shale came under this law, and more than 30,000 claims were filed. After that, shale oil was considered a mineral to be leased to individuals, not to be owned by them. Several other changes in the law followed, and today the government is busy straightening out legal tangles left over from the past.

Optimistic predictions say that, if everything moves along well, by 1985 something like 900,000 barrels of shale oil a day could be taken.

However, no one should think this is an uncomplicated answer to our oil-for-energy needs. Reserves of oil shale are not limitless. And each barrel of oil produced from shale creates nearly a ton and a half of waste matter. A tremendous disposal problem would have to be solved!

7. Everyone Wants to Go Somewhere

Years ago a popular song put to music the thought, "There is no place like home." But after autos and airplanes were invented, people seemed to enjoy traveling far more than staying in one place. It became commonplace to drive a hundred miles over a weekend, or to fly across the continent or to Europe for a short sightseeing trip, or to explore national parks by bus or car.

Unfortunately all such activities take energy. Not just people-energy, but the energy of natural resources. And besides the energy demands for fun travel, there is daily commuting to work, to shop, or do anything that involves going more than a few blocks from home. The easiest way seems: Use the car!

But people are beginning to wonder. They wonder when they find themselves in four or six lanes of slow-moving traffic. They wonder when they see miles of beautiful countryside destroyed by bulldozers so that more highways can be built. They wonder when they are told gasoline supplies are so low each family may be allowed only a limited number of gallons, and prices sky-rocket.

A few of many statistics available are enough to show the increasing drain on natural resources caused by all this travel:

In 1970 the demand for gasoline in the United States was less than six million barrels a day; three years later it was close to seven million. The prediction is that close to eight million barrels a day will be called for by 1976.

During the past fifty years the population of the United States has doubled. In that time the number of automobiles on the road has increased by 800 per cent! There is a car on the road for every two people in the country. Every year motor vehicle travel in the United States adds up to more than a trillion miles.

The amounts of gasoline and oil used for all this driving are tremendous. Still, it is only part of the claim that motor vehicles make on our natural resources. Motor vehicles must have highways to run on!

We can gain a rough idea of the energy that building highways absorbs from a program worked out to provide new roads over a ten-year period. Financing came from federal road-building funds and funds provided by state, county, and city governments.

The construction involved these amounts of resources: 15 billion gallons of gasoline, oil, and grease, for such equipment as earth-moving machinery, billions of tons of assorted materials produced from bituminous coal, millions of barrels of cement—the manufacture of which required billions of kilowatt hours of electrical energy, and more billions of gallons of oil in direct heat.

If such a program settled transportation problems for a long period of time, it might seem worth all this spending of energy. But the discouraging fact is that, even as the highways were being constructed, millions of additional cars were put into use, and demands were begun to turn four-lane highways into six, eight, or ten lanes.

Another discouraging truth is that the constant use of motor vehicles has been creating destructive pollution of the air, harming us not only by directly injuring our health, but by threatening the energy of our total environment. It is harmful to vegetation, it damages crops, and it causes illness among livestock. Left unchecked, it can destroy the complex system on which life depends.

What will solve the serious problems involving transportation, natural resources and health?

First, people must give up the happy idea that our "rich" land has the means to supply everyone's needs and wishes forever and ever. And they should realize that transportation—largely the movement of people and goods by automobile and truck—takes 25 per cent of all the energy consumed in the United States. They should study possibilities for travel other than by automobile.

A number of suggestions are being made, some extremely simple, others requiring a whole new era in the construction of vehicles and tracks.

Almost too obvious to mention as a helpful change in habits is to walk instead of driving. Yet walking in cities, suburbs, or even in the country is not always easy. It is often dangerous because no safe and suitable places are provided for pedestrians. The same problem exists for bicycle riders.

Recommendations have been made to improve this situation: bike lanes and pedestrian zones, for example, should be constructed both in cities and in many country areas. Bike stands should be included in new buildings and added to already existing apartment houses, schools and commercial buildings. Car-free zones should be

When a four-line highway is constructed, it is not unusual for plans to immediately begin for widening it into six, eight, or more lanes. (Wide World Photos)

A number of ideas are being worked on, trying to find new, efficient types of mass transportation. Such a train as this could comfortably carry four hundred passengers. (Ewing Galloway)

created in cities, or streets should be closed to motor vehicles for certain periods, during which time they would be safe for pedestrians and bike riders.

Ecologists are making recommendations, also, about the control of highways. They say in rural areas new highways should not be constructed unless it can be proved that mass transit could not eliminate the need for them. Also, they say, in cities new highways should not be constructed unless every possibility for mass transit has been investigated and developed.

Mass transit moves many people in a vehicle instead of a few or, perhaps, only one person. There are subways that do the job in cities, running underneath streets and avenues. There are buses that go from one city to another, or from place to place within one city's limits, or on cross-country trips. There are railroads. There are airplanes.

Some of these means of travel, once popular, have largely been replaced by the automobile. People shy away from subways which have become dirty, noisy, and overcrowded. And they won't consider using buses because it is inconvenient to reach a bus stop; buses often do not run at scheduled times; and there is no shelter for riders who must wait until a bus comes. The upkeep of railroad trains, tracks, and stations has been neglected until, in a number of places, rail transportation is unattractive and even unsafe.

The answers given to all complaints about such conditions usually revolved around the same problem—money shortage. Yet a Highway Trust Fund of the federal budget has been giving seven billions of dollars, or more, each year for the development of highways. Only a very small amount was allowed to help mass transit. Finally, in the summer of 1973, a long-overdue decision by the government changed this policy so that much greater assistance is being given to railways, subways and bus lines.

A number of highly successful mass transit systems show what can be done. Paris, Montreal, Mexico City, and Moscow all have subway systems that people are actually happy to use.

Today in the United States a number of interesting inventions are being discussed. Among them are "dial-a-bus" arrangements to furnish more personal bus service within cities, and trains that carry not only passengers but the passengers' automobiles as well, and others that carry trucks. There is an automatic, electrically controlled personal "rapid-transit" system where passengers are whisked to their stations at the push of a button. There are moving sidewalks, shuttle trains running on specially built guideways, and monorails suspended overhead.

Some of the innovations are already in operation, others are in an experimental stage. Yet along with the new ideas, the railroad is not to be forgotten. In efficiency, in moving people and freight, when compared mile for mile with other means of transportation, it has an excellent rating.

Good thinking has been shown by a manufacturer who wants to improve the usefulness of bicycles. His new style has four wheels, a windshield and roof, and a mechanical arrangement that allows easier pedaling. Bikes are no longer considered toys. They are an important means of transportation.

There is also a new "people-powered" vehicle for adults that resembles a mini-sportscar, with bucket-type seats for two and a three-speed transmission. It requires no fuel; its power comes from one or two riders using a very efficient pedaling system.

Another example of new thinking is a rival for the snowmobile— an invention that is creating an additional drain on gasoline supplies

*A new trend in transportation is for autos and their drivers, as well as trucks, to
be moved over long distances on railroad tracks rather than on highways.*
(Ewing Galloway)

as well as adding to air pollution. Now a manufacturer is producing a one-dog sled, made of light wood and runners of polyester. Its power (not included with the sale of a sled!) must come from a dog that weighs forty or more pounds.

A fine example of energy conservation and protection of the environment is to be found in a picturesque village at the foot of the Matterhorn in Switzerland. The citizens were asked to vote on a bill that would permit the building of a highway, bringing many additional tourists—and more money—to their shops. Their answer was, "No." Visitors could come on the little railway already existing or not come at all.

8. Atoms, Minerals, and Energy

Someone looking for a source of energy might not be impressed with a certain kind of rock called pitchblende. Yet pitchblende represents a most exciting aspect of energy possibilities; it is in pitchblende that uranium often is found. And the splitting of uranium atoms certainly must be considered the news of the century so far as energy goes.

Unfortunately when the general public first heard about atom splitting, it was in connection with a destructive force—the atomic bombs used near the end of World War II. But atom splitting can be used also to create atomic fuel, which is an almost miraculous advance in producing energy for peaceful purposes.

Man's understanding of uranium as a unique element began only forty years ago. Uranium was known long before that, but no one had realized what its possibilities were.

Then a scientist, Enrico Fermi, tried a number of experiments with the hope of making atoms that would be heavier than uranium atoms. When he shot neutrons at uranium he succeeded; small amounts of heavier elements were indeed formed.

When an atomic explosion is set off, the "cloud" that forms is picturesque. But atomic bombs represent the destructive force of atom splitting. (Courtesy of the American Museum of Natural History)

At the same time his experiments brought about an amazing discovery. He found that when the uranium atoms were hit, some of them split in two. This splitting—called "fission"—of an atom had never before been witnessed.

It was noticed, also, that the splitting of uranium atoms created a great amount of heat. (Later it was to be found that one pound of natural uranium can produce as much heat as a thousand tons of coal.) But, for a while, little use was made of the discovery because of the high cost of obtaining neutrons that would be needed to split large quantities of atoms.

In 1939 another important discovery moved this energy story into a new chapter. Frédéric Joliot-Curie found that, because of what we call a "chain reaction," countless neutrons were unnecessary in producing large-scale fission. When a neutron splits an atom, several new neutrons are created. These, in turn, produce fission in more atoms, while creating still more neutrons. This chain-reaction process continues until all the atoms in a piece of uranium have been split. (In terms of heating, we would say, "until the fuel supply is exhausted.")

With these astonishing facts in mind, a number of scientists gave their best efforts to building an apparatus—a "nuclear reactor"—in which nuclear-fission chain reaction could be initiated and controlled. By 1942 they had succeeded.

After World War II a number of small reactors were built, and the heat from them was used to generate electricity. Now several different styles are being built and used.

Today, also, there are other atomic plants where certain light-weight atoms—such as hydrogen and helium—are joined together in the process known as "fusion."

Fusion is more difficult to achieve than the atom-splitting fission. It is usually accomplished by heating the atoms to an extremely high temperature, until the nuclei of the atoms fuse together. Afterward the fusion of atoms creates its own heat, and continues to do so until no fusible atoms remain.

With atomic fission and fusion at work, it might seem the world's

All minerals that contain uranium give off particles called "radiations" that cannot be seen or felt, but can be detected by scientific measuring devices, one of which is shown here. (Courtesy of the American Museum of Natural History)

energy problems should be under control. But unfortunately there are complications.

When fission occurs, the fragments produced are radioactive; they give off radiations which can be extremely dangerous to the environment and to all living things. No satisfactory way of disposing of them is yet known.

With fusion nuclear plants, the liquid, solid, and gaseous wastes and spray from cooling towers are all threats to the environment.

The concern felt by many people regarding danger from atomic plants has resulted in lawsuits being brought by citizen groups devoted to the protection of natural resources. One will serve as an example:

It was charged that at a reactor testing station in Idaho, liquids from the reactor, containing small amounts of radioactive materials, were seeping into the ground, and that this had been going on for several years. Besides, there had been an accidental leak which spilled half a million gallons of highly radioactive liquid wastes into the earth.

Officials in charge of the reactor operations stated that the ground water in the area was not being used, and that the contaminated liquid would be purified by the time it reached rivers and streams. However, the environmentalists claimed that similar situations had been known where such "purification" had not worked out. Furthermore, a number of things such as flooding by heavy rains, an increased population in the general area, or the construction of a dam, could result in water's being tapped closer to the source of pollution than was presently the case. The new supply could be dangerously radioactive.

Not only uranium, but other elements, and minerals also, are associated with energy. We are more likely to think of them as manufacturing materials. However, some are concerned both with creating energy and in creating demands for it. Iron is one of these.

Iron is needed by animals and plants for their development, growth, and strength. At the same time, iron when used in manufactured articles requires the use of enormous amounts of energy.

The discovery that iron is a useful, strong substance was made at least four thousand years ago. Nevertheless it remained quite unimportant until the nineteenth century, when methods were developed for converting iron ore into pig iron and from that into steel. Then an "iron age" was ready to begin.

Today it is difficult to imagine a world without iron and steel. In the United States it has been called "the backbone of the nation."

We can understand the reason for this if we look back little more than a hundred years, when a great industrial development was taking place, with iron and steel making it all possible. Iron trains were beginning to cross the continent on steel tracks. Steel ships were replacing older wooden styles. Not long after, steel girders were forming the skeletons of great buildings, and steel was used for suspension bridges, transmission towers, machines, pipes, cables, and wires.

These products contributed greatly to the energy of our nation and the world; but the amount of energy needed to take iron ore from the earth and process it for a great variety of uses is almost beyond comprehension.

First it must be mined—an operation that may involve scooping the ore from close to the surface of the ground or going deeper down into the earth. Then the ore must be transported to manufacturing plants, which sometimes are a great distance from the mines. There the ore is subjected to great heat so that the iron will melt and be separated from impurities.

Bringing iron out of the earth is a tough job. This drilling is one of the first operations; blasting will follow. (Ewing Galloway)

The melted iron is then ready to be put to work in many ways, including the production of steel. All of the processes require the use of natural resources to furnish heat. Years ago charcoal was burned to melt the ore. Later coke was found to be a better fuel. And in the very successful open-hearth furnaces, gas, tar and oil all created the flaming energy. Still later, electric-current furnaces were sucessfully employed for making high-grade steel.

Besides being concerned with the natural resources needed to bring iron out of the earth and along to the point where it is used in manufacturing, we may wonder about remaining supplies of the iron itself. Do we have an unlimited supply for the coming years?

The latest report made by a government geological survey tells us that the United States currently is importing about 125 millions of tons annually. Hundreds of millions of tons still remain in our country as resources. However, the metallic elements and minerals that have been millions of years in the making cannot be renewed like crops of grain. Once they have been taken from the earth, nothing remains but ugly holes in the ground.

Of course mining must be continued. But it must be done more wisely, using better techniques, so that more low-grade ores can be obtained, and the least possible harm is done to the environment.

An important aid in the conservation of metals is recycling; that is, using them more than once. A number of volunteer organizations and city governments have been doing good work collecting not only metals but paper and glass, for recycling. But efforts on a greater scale are needed, as a program being carried on by a large aluminum company. Several years ago it organized a recycling project, and offered to pay people for bringing in used aluminum cans. Within two years more than 300 million cans had been received, to be converted into sheets of aluminum that could be turned into new cans.

Energy is needed to accomplish this. But it takes only 5 per cent as much as would be needed to work newly mined metal.

Chromium is a vitally important element in making steel hard and tough, and is valued for many other uses. Our country's supplies are low, known resources representing a supply for only four or five years. Therefore we now import hundreds of thousands of tons each year.

Manganese, not so well known to the public as chromium and

aluminum, is of tremendous importance in the manufacture of steel. Although this metal exists in the United States, our native supplies are of poor quality and are difficult to process. The manganese situation is summed up in a government report: "No domestic reserves." Great quantities must be imported each year.

The copper situation is brighter. Resources in the United States are believed sufficient to last forty-five years. It is hoped that by then new deposits and better methods for extracting low-grade supplies will be discovered.

Copper mining not only brings copper into use, it may produce other important minerals. Silver, for example, is often recovered as a by-product. This is fortunate, because silver is in short supply. Its use in photography alone surpasses the annual production of our country, and it is needed also for electrical and other products.

Asbestos and mercury are two important minerals of which we have only scant reserves.

The story of mining in years past is filled with the excitement of people's hopes and efforts and dreams fulfilled. Unfortunately it also contains many elements of greed, where profit to an individual was far more important than concern for future generations.

During the past seventy-five years, more minerals have been mined than were used in thousands of years of previous history. During this time, laws governing the ownership and working of mines were confused or did not exist at all. Under the Mining Act of 1872 a prospector could look for minerals on most public lands that had not been set aside for a definite purpose. If he found something of value, he could file a claim in a county courthouse and go to work. There was no requirement to notify the federal government of his discovery or to pay any sort of fee for it.

The conflicts that often resulted are well known; dramas concerning them can be seen in countless motion pictures and television stories. But the abandoned mines and scarred earth left by people who didn't fully appreciate their treasures are not often shown.

The Mining Act of 1872 was little changed for a hundred years. The only improvement came in 1920 when a leasing act gave some protection to oil and certain other minerals. But the status of the hard-rock minerals stayed the same.

Now other improvements in the laws are being worked on. One states that a prospector will have to file any claim to a mineral discovery with the Federal Bureau of Land Management within a year after it is found. Otherwise it would be declared abandoned. Another change would be that anyone working a mine would have rights only to the mineral deposit, not to the land. In time the land would belong to the government.

Such reforms should help to improve a critical situation. But even with the best of laws, the problems concerned with protecting minerals for future use remain enormous.

9. The Sun — Great, Glorious Power Plant

The hydrogen bomb has been called a small-scale copy of the sun. The comparison makes sense, because the sun's energy results from the fusion of hydrogen into helium. This is the process which takes place in hydrogen bomb explosions.

Of course we prefer to think of solar energy as a constructive force, rather than its destructive possibilities. But two thousand years ago it was used in a battle between two nations. History records how the Greek inventor, Archimedes, used it to destroy a fleet of Roman ships that were about to attack his homeland.

As the ships came close to the shores of Greece, Archimedes set up a number of square mirrors on hinges, placing them in a position so that they directed the sun's rays toward the ships. Soon the heat they generated became so fierce the sails caught fire, and the fleet was reduced to ashes.

This story caused debates through many years, as some people insisted that such an accomplishment would be impossible. However, in 1747 a French scientist named Buffon arranged 168 small mirrors in a position so that they would concentrate rays from the sun on wood, placed more than two hundred feet away. Soon the wood was on fire.

This was considered proof that the Archimedes story was true. Later, it was also demonstrated that lead and silver could be melted by similar means.

Not long after this demonstration, another Frenchman built iron solar furnaces which could smelt iron and copper. They were used with considerable success, not only in France but in Denmark and Persia.

Through the years that followed, there were several interesting developments connected with solar energy, and just a century after Buffon's demonstrations, a number of inventors began working on its possibilities. In the United States and Europe the sun was used to power a variety of engines.

About 1870 a highly effective water system was constructed in South America. It provided fresh water for a parched area of Chile where mining operations were being carried out. For this, ocean water was pumped into long, shallow troughs—50,000 square feet of them. The troughs were covered with slanted panes of glass through which sunlight streamed, heating the water and causing it to evaporate. As evaporation took place, it condensed on the glass covers, leaving its salt behind. From there it ran off into other troughs from which it was drawn as needed. As much as 6,000 gallons of fresh water a day were provided for the little mining town which kept in operation for almost forty years.

Today the shortage of fresh, clean water is as great in many parts of the world as it was so long ago in that mining area of South America. But thus far no great effort is being made to use solar

With this forty-foot-high "solar furnace" set up at the Laboratory of Solar Energy in France, a movable mirror directs the sun's rays to fixed mirrors. Tremendous heat is generated. (Ewing Galloway)

energy to supply the needs. On a small scale, though, it has become a lifesaver for people adrift in the ocean after a ship or plane wreck. Sun power is used in a balloonlike device, called a "still," which can be tethered to a lifeboat.

With such equipment, someone in a lifeboat may float the device, after first pouring some sea water into it. The heat of the sun soon evaporates fresh water from this. It condenses on the walls of the still and then runs into a collecting trap, forming a small, but perhaps life saving, reservoir of drinking water.

Though the process of obtaining fresh water through sun power is important, it is only one of many tremendous possibilities solar energy has to offer. We may wonder why more has not been done with it till now.

The explanation, in a word, could be: money.

Early in the present century when one experiment after another involving solar energy was carried out successfully, fossil fuels were plentiful and cheap. And oil, coal, and gas could power all kinds of engines without the complications of learning to use sun power in their place. It was cheaper to continue drilling and mining than to harness energy from the sky.

Fortunately the hopes for solar energy were never allowed to die. A number of private companies and scientific groups kept up a lively interest in how it could be used, and the United Nations encouraged working with it, particularly for helping underdeveloped nations of the world. From time to time a United States senator would propose a large research fund to be set up for federal government work in this field. But until recently such proposals were turned down. Money and attention were being devoted to splitting atoms.

Then came the Space Age.

This began when scientists found that satellites could be made to orbit the earth, and they realized that all kinds of dreams about exploring "outer space," the moon, and distant planets could come true. A great partner in their accomplishments would be solar energy.

The electrical equipment put into the first experimental spacecrafts had been heavy and costly, and lasted a relatively short time. In contrast, solar batteries were small and simple, yet they could continue to generate power as it was needed, performing a variety of functions.

A model of Telstar, shown here, was inspected and tested repeatedly before the actual satellite was completed and launched. This remarkable pioneer in ocean-spanning television, only thirty-four and a half inches in diameter, was equipped with 3,600 solar cells for converting sunlight into energy. (Courtesy Bell Laboratories)

Thanks to solar batteries, one fantastic invention followed another. A weather satellite, making possible global weather forecasting, was one. Then Telstar, powered by 3,600 solar batteries, became a magnificent satellite making possible world-wide communication through the air.

Meanwhile progress was being made for everyday use of solar energy on the earth. Solar batteries were taking the place of electricity in a number of manufactured articles, including transistor radios, which scored an immediate success. (A solar cell, made of carefully prepared silicon, and exposed to sunlight, behaves much like an electric battery with a positive and negative side.) In 1955 solar cells were even used to run a rural telephone system in Georgia.

Long before solar batteries were coming into general use, solar hot-water systems were quite popular in warmer parts of the United States. There were different styles, but the general idea involved lengths of pipe, painted black, placed on top of a roof, on the southern exposure. The pipes were covered with glass panels through which the sun could shine. As water and pipes became heated, the water would be forced to higher levels in the system and into a storage tank, as unheated water flowed into lower levels.

Solar water heaters have proved efficient and economical. Today solar heat serves also to bring many swimming pools to a comfortable temperature.

Even more exciting is the news of homes and other buildings being heated, and cooled, by the sun. A number of them have been constructed, but they have been regarded as novelties rather than the beginning of a new trend.

But now, in the mid-1970s, acceptance of the idea of solar heating is becoming widespread. At an international conference sponsored by the United Nations in 1973, one builder reported that his firm was constructing ten solar-energy apartments in Vermont and office buildings in New Hampshire and Michigan. Such buildings will be air-conditioned, as well as heated, with sun power.

Another prospect is for "solar farms." The idea is to have pipes containing a mixture of chemicals lying across twenty-five square miles of desert. Heated by the sun, the chemicals would produce steam, and this would power turbines which, in turn, would produce electricity.

So effective. So clean. So available. Again a question: Why is solar energy taking so long to become widely used? And again the answer is: money.

Sunshine comes to us without cost, but to construct solar-energy buildings is far more expensive than to build the kind that use coal, oil, or gas. However, two developments—the specter of an energy crisis and a growing pollution problem—have been changing the public's attitude about what expenses are worth while.

Fossil fuels, in spite of all efforts at prevention, still pollute our air and waters. And with our supplies of natural resources shrinking, we must thoroughly investigate any possible source of additional energy.

Some private companies have been doing spectacular work in harnessing the sun's energy, notably Bell Telephone Laboratories, which developed Telstar, and the Radio Corporation of America, which pioneered in weather satellites. A number of other companies also are contributing. But because research, experiments, and construction work on a large scale are so costly, progress demands the co-operation of government.

Happily, it has begun. We now find in our federal annual budget some funds devoted to solar studies, and several proposals are being considered by Congress to increase the government's commitment. One is the creation of a Solar Energy Data Bank which would serve as a clearinghouse for all vital information related to the development of solar energy.

10. The Good Earth

Fertile soil was one of the greatest gifts America had to offer early settlers from Europe. It was not found everywhere. In the area where Plymouth, Massachusetts, was to develop, Pilgrims could not raise enough crops to prevent hunger and loss of energy. Only corn, brought from a distance away, and sea food kept the colony from failing.

It was a different story when settlers moved along through the Connecticut Valley. Rich meadowlands awaited them there; the crops they planted grew as if touched by magic. When more Europeans pushed farther to the west, they found as good, or even better, soil. Pennsylvania soon became the granary of the colonies. By the time of the American Revolution, many families had moved along, on foot and with wagons, to Kentucky and Tennessee territory —all anxious to get a section of that beautiful land for themselves.

But gradually a change came over many of these people who at first fully appreciated the good soil. They took on more land than they could handle, they used it recklessly, and they let it wash away.

A tragic scene, repeated many times in the Midwest, shows the result of land abuse. Good topsoil was replaced by dust—an agricultural disaster. (Wide World Photos)

With proper care, ruined farmlands may be made productive again. This wheat is growing on a once-devastated farm in Oklahoma. (Wide World Photos)

Their answer to the failing crops that resulted was to move farther west.

If America had remained sparsely settled, such abuses to the soil could have continued for centuries without the continent's being seriously damaged. However, once immigration to the New World began, there was no slowing down, and the results of land abuse soon began to show. Even in Colonial Days some enlightened men such as George Washington and Thomas Jefferson looked into the future and saw trouble if land was not protected. But they received little support. The public liked to think that abundant good soil would last forever.

Pioneering to the west continued, and by 1890 the American frontier had disappeared; the continent had been settled from coast to coast.

Nevertheless, there were still great, open spaces, with many of the "spaces" fertile, and apparently quite perfect for agriculture. Farmers enthusiastically dug in! In countless acres where native vegetation had flourished, they plowed and planted wheat. Then they plowed again and again. Within fifty years the plains of western Kansas, Oklahoma, and Texas had been plowed once too often and the soil had turned to dust. In 1933 when prairie winds swept over the land, there was nothing to hold it.

The dust began to blow. It spiraled upward for thousands of feet, and moved along with the wind for hundreds of miles. The dust storms could be seen from cities along the Atlantic coast, and even for hundreds of miles out to sea.

These devastating storms did not end with 1933. They continued during the three years that followed, and people were no longer unbelieving when leaders talked in the manner of Washington and

Jefferson. They were frightened. They wanted action to help restore the earth's richness.

Soon several federal programs dealing with soil control and conservation, including a Soil Conservation Service, were established. Farmers were encouraged to plow in ways that would keep erosion down to the smallest possible degree, were shown how planting win-

A farmer tried to free his small tractor, bogged down in three feet of dust, as a March wind swept across Kansas. Farmlands soon looked like deserts. (Wide World Photos)

ter crops would prevent the damage that would occur if soil was left bare for a season, and were told how the land would benefit from mulching. How to choose suitable planting grounds was explained. The planting of trees and shrubs around farmlands was advised to form barriers against wind and to allow their roots to hold on to the soil.

The roots of a tree can reach down like giant fingers, gripping the earth. Big roots and small ones help to prevent soil from being washed or blown away. (Courtesy of the American Museum of Natural History)

But in spite of all the improved agricultural practices, erosion goes on. Government studies show that many hundreds of millions of tons of sediment run off the land into our rivers and streams each year. This loss to the land is no gain for the water. There it becomes a serious pollutant. Even the use of great hydroelectric facilities can be destroyed by sediment.

Inefficient planting is by no means the only enemy from which soil suffers. Building developments, made up of homes and industrial plants, have been constructed on some of our finest, most fertile soil. The owners of such land have been allowed to sell it without any restrictions as to its use. And not many people have been putting consideration for the earth above money to be made by profitable land transactions.

Roadbuilding is another part of the destructive chain as woodlands and meadows are uprooted and replaced by miles of concrete. With each heavy rain, then, water pours over the highways, and flooding at the sides washes away still more soil.

In the 1970s floods have had a devasting effect on small farms of New England. The rivers of Pennsylvania on various occasions have raged out of control, and the mighty Mississippi has flooded millions of acres of fine farmland.

A survey reveals that in the eastern United States the original eight inches of good topsoil have dwindled to an average five inches.

Soil that has been robbed of its valuable nutrients can be renewed if it is cared for and fed chemical and natural fertilizers. But not if the abuse goes on for too long a time; then the process of destruction cannot be reversed. At best, it takes more than a person's lifetime to restore any that has been badly damaged.

Trends in farming are changing, with small farms giving way to large-scale operations. When the Soil Conservation Service was established in 1935, the average size was 150 acres. About thirty years later the average size had been increased to more than 300 acres. Today, predictions are that by the year 2000, the average farm will be well over 1,000 acres. But no matter on what scale agricultural projects—or other kinds of developments—are carried out, one thing is certain. We need to make the best possible use of our land!

11. Wood and Forests

Redwood trees and giant sequoias may grow for well over a thousand years. Some are known to have lived more than two thousand. Such trees may well be considered irreplaceable, and we treasure them as heirlooms.

Fortunately we do not have to wait this long for many kinds of trees to reach their full growth. And forests, if properly handled, can be kept as a resource to be regularly used and renewed.

Today, a number of enlightened lumber companies are actually tree farmers. When "harvesting," they plant as many, or more, trees than are cut. And processes have been developed so that every bit of cut wood, from heavy lumber to sawdust, can be put to some good purpose.

Of all our natural resources, nothing has gone through more drastic changes, since Europeans began to settle in America, than forests. When settlers first arrived, they found a seemingly endless supply of trees, and quickly began to cut them down, using the wood to build homes, fences, and furniture, and for heating purposes.

Wood also was a valuable source of energy. It was the fuel for fireplaces, and later for furnaces. It was used for power in manufacturing plants before coal or other fossil fuels were available. When lumber was sent to be sold in Europe, it was conveyed on wooden ships, powered by wood-burning furnaces.

Later, as railroads helped to move people westward, the energy of burning wood moved the trains. And lumber formed the foundation on which to lay steel tracks.

By then incredible destruction of trees had taken place. In New England white pines were all but wiped out. Then armies of ax-wielding woodsmen tackled the forests of New York, Pennsylvania, Ohio, and Indiana. Later southern and western forests were under similar attack.

Apparently there were no regrets about destroying this wealth of trees. For years the people feared, and even hated, the forests in which dangerous animals and hostile Indians might be concealed, and which took up land that otherwise could be used for farming.

Often those who cleared trees from the land did not bother to stack logs for later use. Instead they kept great open fires burning

In some parts of the world, wood is still important as fuel, but in the United States it is used chiefly as lumber. These logs in Michigan are being showered before going into a sawmill. (Ewing Galloway)

83

Logging on a small scale may still operate with real "horsepower" rather than depending on machines. (Ewing Galloway)

With this machine, two men can plant thousands of trees a day. The machine splits the soil to a depth of about ten inches, and lets it fall back into place after the young trees have been dropped. (Ewing Galloway) in a field on which to throw newly cut lumber. Some such bonfires were kept burning continually for two or three years.

It was not until late in the nineteenth century that people began to realize the bountiful American tree supply was not limitless. Then suddenly there was a distressed cry, "Timber famine!" In spite of new sources of energy and building and manufacturing materials, no one wanted to face the prospect of a country without forests.

By 1900 a real effort was begun to protect them, and in recent years the federal government's Forest Service (a branch of the Department of Agriculture) has been keeping a close watch on their needs. Protection of many kinds is called for.

Probably the forest "enemy" we think of first is fire. We can see the trees explode in flames, and great flames sweep over beautiful woodlands in a matter of minutes. We know that countless wild animals are dead or homeless after such a disaster, and small plants and humus are burned off the forest floor.

About three million acres of American forests are destroyed by fires each year. About 90 per cent of them are caused by human carelessness.

Forests need protection, too, from disease and insects. The American chestnut tree, which once provided fine hardwood lumber, has now all but vanished. It was killed by a fungus disease which is believed to have been brought to the United States on lumber imported from Asia about 1900. A few years later, the chestnut trees in New York State began to die, and within the next thirty years, nearly every chestnut tree in North America was gone.

Today many trees, and entire woodlands, are suffering from a gypsy moth menace. This insect was imported from Europe to New England in 1869 by a man who hoped that in its caterpillar stage it would be able to produce silk as the oriental silk worms did. The

*A small fire,
started in dry
leaves, can result
in the destruction
of beautiful
woodlands,
valuable timber,
and the homes of
countless animals.*
(Ewing Galloway)

only result was a plague for our native trees, for some of his moths escaped. Their descendants multiplied into the millions, and now they are a serious pest throughout our eastern forests.

Still another type of forest destruction comes about through the building of highways and dams. Mighty trees fall under bulldozers, to be replaced by concrete. Dams storing small oceans of water cause trees to be flooded. Natural disasters such as hurricanes and earthquakes can cause the death of countless trees with one blow.

We find, therefore, that in spite of the good work that is being done, we cannot relax with the comforting thought that our remaining forests are now safe for all time. Hazards still threaten and are sure to continue.

In some parts of the world wood is still valued as a fuel, but in the United States we no longer depend on it for direct energy. However, the earth has need of forests as much as it ever did. Their leafy green canopies have a healthy effect on the soil under them and the air around them. The tree roots hold the soil firmly, preventing its being washed or blown away.

Forests and even small woodlands make life possible for many kinds of animals. Without the protective covering and the food supplies they offer, countless mammals, birds, reptiles, and insects would disappear forever.

12. What Can We Do with a Crisis?

A crisis calls for clear, honest thinking and for positive action. And the best time to think about one is before it explodes with destructive force.

Like it or not, we must admit an energy crisis is at hand, and laws are now being passed to control it. But when a slight easing of worry over shortages begins, people are likely to relax into wasteful habits. They will choose, mistakenly, to believe that energy shortages are caused only by war or political maneuvering, and that when such tragedies end, abundant fuels will be available.

Another danger lies in becoming too optimistic over reports about new sources of energy such as nuclear and solar energy. We must realize that undoubtedly years will pass before such innovations can safely supply the world's needs. And we have to remember that, at its present rate of growth, the world's population in only fifty years will be more than ten *billion* people. The United States alone every year has an additional two million people who must have food, clothing, and shelter.

As we see enormous energy problems in the making, it might seem only the government and large industries can do anything about them. But such is not the case. A booklet recently published by the Environmental Protection Agency of the United States is called, *Don't Leave It All to the Experts,* and this is a good motto for citizens everywhere.

Look at the transportation problem. It is recognized that trains are a valuable means of transportation. Nevertheless they have long been neglected, and when they were criticized, the answer often was to abandon services altogether.

This was about to happen with a rail line in New York State; but one citizen decided to fight. Lottie Gay Carson had been protesting for years against the cutback on commuter trains from New York City to her home town. It had done no good, but when the rail line tried to end freight traffic service, she began a real campaign.

Supported by businessmen, farmers, and other commuters of the area, Mrs. Carson brought a suit against the railroad. Her lawyer showed that trucks—which would have to take over if the train service was given up—would use up to five times as much energy as trains to handle the same load. It was also pointed out that increasing truck traffic would increase air pollution, and that the change-over in transportation would increase grain and dairy prices. The judge ruled in favor of Mrs. Carson's case—and the trains rolled on!

Look at the highway problem. In a number of areas, new or expanded highways have been built without their having been proved necessary. Some of them cut across fields and woodlands while others go into heavily populated cities, already a maze of roads for auto traffic.

This was the case in Washington, D.C., in 1968, when a new freeway was planned to run through a residential district. Mrs. Helen Leavitt, whose home would have been directly in its path, led other citizens in a legal battle showing that the additional road was not needed, and would actually do more harm than good. The case was so decided, and the freeway construction was stopped.

Look at the electric problem. Here every citizen has an opportunity to help avoid an energy crisis by not being wasteful. The millions of heating and cooling systems used in the United States consume huge amounts of electric energy. Strangely, people often keep their homes (and public places, such as markets, restaurants, and theaters) colder in the summer than they wish them to be in winter. In other words, electricity is wasted to bring summer temperatures below a comfortable level while in the winter, thermostats are turned up to an unhealthy, overheated degree.

Another important way to control waste in the heating or cooling of buildings is to take care with their construction. If a good job is done on insulation, the heated or cooled air does not seep out.

Electricity can be wasted, too, in sinks and tubs, for running water requires electricity to be pumped from its source to a faucet. Therefore wasting water—even cold water—wastes electricity.

The varieties of electric appliances today are almost endless, but if used wisely, they need not be criticized. Dishwashers and clothes washers, for example should be operated only for full loads, and refrigerators and freezers should be opened only when necessary.

Look at recycling efforts. This is an activity that can be carried out on a small scale as well as large. Many communities and private industries are encouraging people to bring such reusable materials as paper, glass and aluminum to collecting stations. Every such program, if well run, is a help.

A fine program is being carried on to recycle aluminum, with cans being collected at the rate of two million a month. (Photo courtesy Alcoa)

The federal Bureau of Mines is increasing efforts to put metal from scrap autos and discarded household appliances back to work. The city dumps of our nation are said to hold more than five million tons of iron, and a million tons of assorted metals. Such scrap can become a "new" natural resource.

Look at ways to obtain new energy. Windmills may not seem new; they have been used for a long time in Holland to pump water from the dikes back into the sea. And farmers in our own Midwest have used them instead of electricity to pump their water.

But this has been use of wind power on a relatively small scale. Now, serious attempts are being made to manufacture and store hydrogen—a valuable energy source—by using windmills of ultra-scientific design.

Ideas for harnessing the power of tides have been around for a long time, but only about fifty operations in the world have been really successful. Certain conditions are necessary, such as an irregular shoreline, with partially enclosed small bays, and a great range between low and high tides. However, the possibilities of further power to be supplied by the ebb and flow of the ocean are worth continued exploration.

"Natural" heat is another interesting possibility. This is the energy found where volcanic forces have left reservoirs of heat, together with dissolved minerals and water, trapped in the earth. Harnessing such energy—known as "geothermal"—has proved of considerable value in New Zealand and Iceland, and it seems to have possibilities for our country.

Look at auto use. Car pools for people driving to work or school can mean important savings of gas. Where bicycle riding or walking is safe, or buses or trains are available—all may save gas that would be needed for travel by car.

There are ways to be saving of gas even as we drive. One is to travel no faster than fifty or fifty-five miles per hour on highways. (Such limitations have recently been made a nationwide law.) Limiting the use of air conditioners and any "power" accessories that consume fuel are also helpful efforts. The use of small cars rather than heavy models is an important saving.

According to our Department of the Interior, 70 per cent of all gasoline used in the United States is absorbed by the automobile.

The government is taking notice of our "disappearing" energy in a number of ways. Newly created offices in the Department of the Interior have the responsibility of studying and co-ordinating energy

When safe routes are provided for bicycle riding, this means of transportation can be useful as well as fun. (Edward N. Stiso Photo)

policies on a nationwide scale, of carrying on research and development, and of enforcing laws designed to protect all natural resources.

These departments will have a difficult job at best. To be successful, they will need the co-operation of industry and citizens—in fact, of all who consume energy. And this means everyone.

93

Index

DOROTHY E. SHUTTLESWORTH has taken an active interest in conservation since she began working at The American Museum of Natural History in New York at the age of seventeen. There she was editor of *Junior Natural History Magazine* for a dozen years, during which time she began writing books for young people. Her family includes her husband, Melvin Shuttlesworth, a son, Gregory, who is an economist, specializing in energy concerns with a leading New York financial institution, and a daughter, Lee Ann, who worked with her mother on DISAPPEARING ENERGY. Mrs. Shuttlesworth is one of the founders of New Jersey Citizens for Clean Air, Inc.

LEE ANN WILLIAMS received a B.S. degree from the University of Kentucky, and is now teaching science at the Intermediate School of East Orange, New Jersey.